DITS and DAHS

The A B C 's of
Morse Code Operating

BY ED TOBIAS, KR3E

CQ Communications, Inc.

Library of Congress Catalog Number: 2017930750
ISBN: 0-943016-54-1

Editor: Gail Sheehan, K2RED
Layout and Production: Elizabeth Ryan and Dorothy Kehrwieder
Cover Photo: Richard Moseson, W2VU

Published by CQ Communications, Inc.
17 West John Street
Hicksville, New York 11801 USA

Printed in the United States of America

Acknowledgments

This book wouldn't have been possible without the help of several of my CW friends who have shared their knowledge and pictures. I've had the pleasure of shaking hands with a few, but I recognize most only by the sound of their "fists."

Suggestions about key adjustments came from Marshall, N1FN (with pictures), James, WB8SIW and Don, WB6BEE.

Pictures of some vintage keys came from Fabio, IK0IXI.

Pictures of mobile and portable set-ups were provided by Red, K5ALU, Patrick, WW9R, Mike, W0VTT, Paul, G6PZ, Bob, N1RA, John, K1JD, Mike, AD5A and Robert, S53R. Red, Paul, Bob and John added some great operating and set-up suggestions.

Thanks to John, ON4UN and Mark, ON4WW for allowing me to use an excerpt from their excellent publication *Ethics and Operating Procedures for the Radio Amateur.*

Finally, a thank you to Gail, K2RED, who edited this content over a difficult year.

DITS and DAHS

The A B C .'s of Morse Code Operating

By Ed Tobias, KR3E

In the Beginning

When many of today's CW operators got their first ham ticket, they had no choice; you had to learn Morse code to obtain a ham radio license. In the U.S., five words a minute was the requirement for the entry level Novice license and for the renewable, but VHF only, Technician. It was 13 wpm for a General or an Advanced class and 20 wpm for an Extra. Taking a higher class exam required appearing before an FCC examiner and demonstrating that you could send and receive one minute of solid copy at the appropriate speed using a straight hand key. There were similar CW requirements in other countries.

In 1991 the CW requirement was eliminated for the Technician license. In 2000 the speed was reduced to 5 wpm for all of the other classes of license and on Feb. 23, 2007 the code requirement was eliminated entirely. At the time of that decision the Federal Communications Commission wrote "…the FCC believes that the public interest is not served by requiring facility in Morse Code when the trend in amateur communications is to use voice and digital technologies for exchanging messages….This change eliminates an unnecessary regulatory burden that may discourage current amateur radio operators from advancing their skills and participating more fully in the benefits of amateur radio."

However, you bought this book, so you must have some interest in learning or improving your CW operating. That's great!

Twelve Reasons to Read Further

1. CW gets through. Every day, even in the worst band conditions, CW operators are working rare DX using only 100 watts and wire antennas–and sometimes even less. A CW signal can have a 10 to 20 dB advantage over SSB. Since

every 6 dB increase in your signal results in an increase of one S-unit on the receiving station's S-meter, a CW signal should be about two S-units louder than an SSB signal running the same power and using the same antenna.

2. It's easy to exchange basic information no matter what language each station operator speaks. Standard abbreviations, similar to what kids use when they text, convey the same meaning whether you're a W, DK, JA, or YV.

3. Learning CW is a fun challenge!

4. There are so many different types of keys made that your "fist" (sending hand), and brain, will never get bored.

5. You can pack a rig in a backpack, hike up a mountain peak, and start a pileup.

6. Some DXpeditions concentrate on CW. A few are *exclusively* CW.

7. It's easier to break through a pileup.

8. You can't count on code readers to get it right.

9. It's the only way to work earth-moon-earth (EME).

10. In an emergency you don't need a microphone. Shorting two pieces of wire on and off can create a CW signal.

11. In many contests a CW contact counts three times as much as an SSB QSO, and some contests are CW only.

12. Off the air, you and your friends can whistle secret messages to each other.

If that's not enough, read how Dr. Dennis Ross, N6DR describes the *magic* of CW in the March 1992 issue of *QST* magazine:

> *There's a special nature to communications via Morse code. At night when I wear headphones and listen to code over the shortwave radio (usually with my eyes closed), I feel that I'm communicating without talking or hearing voices. After a long day of talking to people and hearing many voices, it's a pleasant feeling. An hour or so after I put on the headphones and Morse code fills my ears I have the feeling that I'm using a more primitive part of my brain. The message seems to come to me in a whisper or even to represent something I'm remembering rather than hearing. I no longer formulate what I want to say and then translate it into code for my fingers to send. The thoughts just come out... This doesn't surprise me. Morse code is a social equalizer and a more intimate way of talking.*
>
> (Copyright the American Radio Relay League, ARRL)

Are you ready for that intimate on the air experience? Read on!

Table of Contents

Chapter 1

First Things First

"The secret to becoming a proficient CW Operator: Make CW a second language" – **WØUCE (SK)**

OK, let's start you on your way to CW fluency. When many of today's CW operators learned the code they did it one letter at a time. Some of us even used 3x5 flash-cards to help memorize each letter. If we were lucky we had a mentor, known in ham-talk as an "Elmer," to teach us the basics. After getting our ham ticket we went onto the Novice bands (portions of several HF bands to which Novice licensees were restricted) to practice our newly learned skills with other newly minted hams, all of us with shaky fists and copying one letter at a time with pencil and paper.

Today, learning CW, or increasing your speed, is much easier. There are on-line programs, many of them free, that can teach you the code or help you increase your speed off the air. There is even a free, structured, multi-week course taught by Elmers from an international CW club (see below). It combines off-air and on-air instruction.

Unlike years ago, much of today's CW instruction teaches students to recognize letters that are sent at relatively fast speeds and then students quickly progress to learning full words, rather than single letters. The goal is to have a student copy words in his (or her) head, rather than writing down letters, as quickly as possible.

This is a good time to talk about dits and dahs. A "dit" is the *sound* of a dot. A "dah" is the *sound* of a dash. A dah is three times longer than a dit.

When you're learning the letters, numbers, and other Morse code characters, you need to be thinking in sounds. The letter "E" is "dit." The letter "A" is "di-dah."

A di-dah	N dah-dit
B dah-di-di-dit	O dah-dah-dah
C dah-di-dah-dit	P di-dah-dah-dit
D dah-di-dit	Q dah-dah-di-dah
E dit	R di-dah-dit
F di-di-dah-dit	S di-di-dit
G dah-dah-dit	T dah
H di-di-di-dit	U di-di-dah
I di-dit	V di-di-di-dah
J di-dah-dah-dah	W di-dah-dah
K dah-di-dah	X dah-di-di-dah
L di-dah-di-dit	Y dah-di-dah-dah
M dah-dah	Z dah-dah-di-dit

1 di-dah-dah-dah-dah	6 dah-di-di-di-dit
2 di-di-dah-dah-dah	7 dah-dah-di-di-dit
3 di-di-di-dah-dah	8 dah-dah-dah-di-dit
4 di-di-di-di-dah	9 dah-dah-dah-dah-dit
5 di-di-di-di-dit	0 dah-dah-dah-dah-dah

Period (AAA)	di-dah-di-dah-di-dah
Question mark (IMI)	di-di-dah-dah-di-dit
Comma (MIM)	dah-dah-di-di-dah-dah

When copying CW you want to be able to recognize the *sound* of a letter, rather than trying to count the dots and dashes for each letter as it's sent. When I send my name, you want to hear "dit dah-di-dit" and recognize that you heard "Ed". If you take the time to count "dot" and "dash dot dot" the other station will be three letters down the road before you've finished counting those two.

Once you understand this concept you're ready to check out some places to help you begin to learn, or improve, your CW language skills. And, best of all, they're free!

There's a Web Site or a Club for That

The CW Academy
(www.cwops.org/cwacademy2.html)

Volunteers from the CW Operators club take students through three levels of twice-weekly classes, beginning with a level for those who know no code and progressing to speeds of better than 20 words per minute. Classes begin off the air, using Skype audio/video, and progress to on-air sessions. Students begin by learning all of the Morse letters and numbers sent at a letter-speed of about 20 wpm. They move on to learning how to hold a QSO, how to participate in a contest and in a DX pileup - good, real-world stuff. At higher levels students improve their head-copying skills at faster speeds using a combination of Internet and on-air classes. Classes run for eight weeks at each level and are held three times a year. There's a waiting list, so sign up quickly.

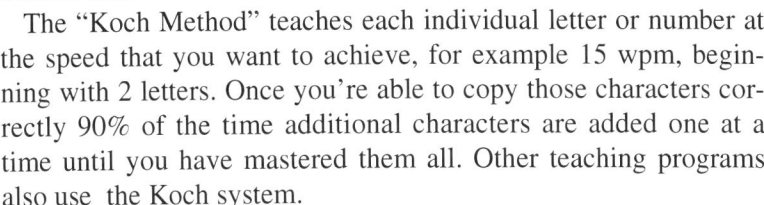

The CW Academy uses a combination of two CW teaching methods: Koch and Farnsworth.

The "Koch Method" teaches each individual letter or number at the speed that you want to achieve, for example 15 wpm, beginning with 2 letters. Once you're able to copy those characters correctly 90% of the time additional characters are added one at a time until you have mastered them all. Other teaching programs also use the Koch system.

The "Farnsworth Method" is Koch with longer spaces between the letters. Like Koch, characters are sent at the speed that you want to achieve. To make copying easier, however, the spaces between the characters are longer than normal.

Morse Code Trainer
(http://.morsecode.scphillips.com/trainer)

This web site is used by CW Academy students to practice copying and sending Morse code, and it matches what's being taught in each CWA session. The free program also can be downloaded.

FISTS Code Buddies
(http://fistsna.org/codebuddy.html)

Whether or not you participate in a formal CW teaching program, it will be an immense help to have an Elmer give you one-on-one assistance. The FISTS CW Club, which is dedicated to promoting Morse code around the world, can hook you up with an Elmer to help you improve your on-air CW. There's also a wealth of basic information for CW beginners on the club's web site.

G4FON's Morse Trainer

(www.g4fon.net)

This is free Window's software, written by Ray, G4FON, and is recommended by lots of CW blogs and web sites. I agree with them. It's a very good teaching tool.

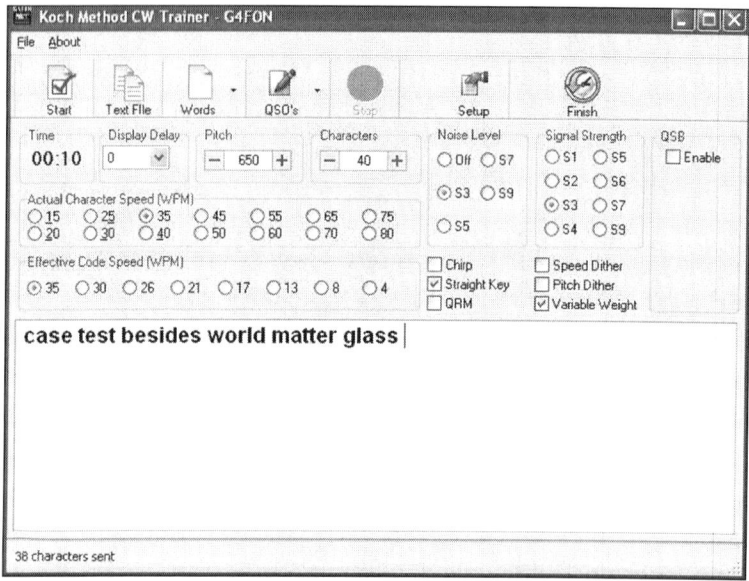

Morse trainer uses the Koch method to teach basic CW. Then, once you have the basics down, you can select between different words, text files, and QSO formats to increase your speed at your own pace. As you improve your skills, Morse Trainer gives you the option of adding in QRM, QRN, QSB, and selecting the received signal strength ...all of the problems you might encounter in a real, on-air QSO. The program also allows you to adjust both the speed at which the characters are sent and, separately, the spacing between the characters. As this book was being written in mid-2016, Ray was updating his program so that you can use it to practice sending, too. An electronic voice speaks a word and you send it back, using a code practice oscillator or the side-tone from your rig in an off-air "test" mode. The program "receives" what you send and it shows you how well you did.

K6RAU Code Course

(www.pdarrl.org/K6RAU/)

This is for the very beginner. The course consists of 12 lessons, each running 30 minutes. The web site promises, "One does not have to know a 'dit' from a 'dah'. Just with paper and pencil in hand, follow the voice instructions." The narrator is Fred, K6DUU (now SK), father of K6RAU.

CW Player
(http://f6dqm.free.fr/software.htm)

This is a free program for Windows, written by F6DQM, which provides practice on letters and word groups similar to the style of the WØUCE method. The CW Academy has incorporated CW Player into some of its classes.

Just Learn Morse Code
(www.justlearnmorsecode.com)

This is also Windows software designed to teach CW to beginners using a combination of the Koch and Farnsworth methods.

Learn CW Online
(http://lcwo.net)

This is a full-service web site, created by Fabian, DJ1YFK. There are basic lessons and practice sessions using code groups, calls, and text with menu-selectable speeds and other features, using the Koch method. It also tracks your progress. The web site is available in more than two dozen languages. Fabian is one of the stars of the high-speed CW world. He is a multi-time winner of the German Cup of High Speed Telegraphy and is a member of the German High Speed Telegraphy Team. (Read more about high-speed CW contesting in Chapter 6).

K9OX's Training Program
(http://c2.com/morse/)

Windows, Mac, Linux, or DOS. This program sends semi-random letters and numbers at variable speeds.

W3TTT CW Practice
(speeds.http://w3ttt.listen2myradio.com)

On-line code practice at 12 wpm using text from Google News.

Morse Runner
(www.dxatlas.com/MorseRunner/)

This Windows software simulates a pileup. The user can set the speed and the number of simultaneous calls and add QRM, QSB, etc. It's a program that I have fun using, when the bands are dead, to pretend that I'm rare DX. This program is used, along with RufzXP (see below), in some high-speed contests.

RufzXP Training Software
(www.rufzxp.net/)

Put your paddle to the metal and zoom to ultra-high-speed with this software, by DL4MM, that sends random calls at speeds that can top 200 wpm! High-speed champion DF1YFK describes the program as a "devilish concept." RufzXP sends a single callsign at an initial speed that's set by the user (as slow as you like). If the call is copied correctly, points are awarded and it sends another callsign at a slightly higher speed. If it's copied *incorrectly*, the speed of the next callsign will be *decreased* and points will be deducted. The default setting for each attempt is 50 callsigns which are randomly selected from a database of real calls. This is excellent practice for hams who are interested in CW contests and it's also simply a lot of fun.

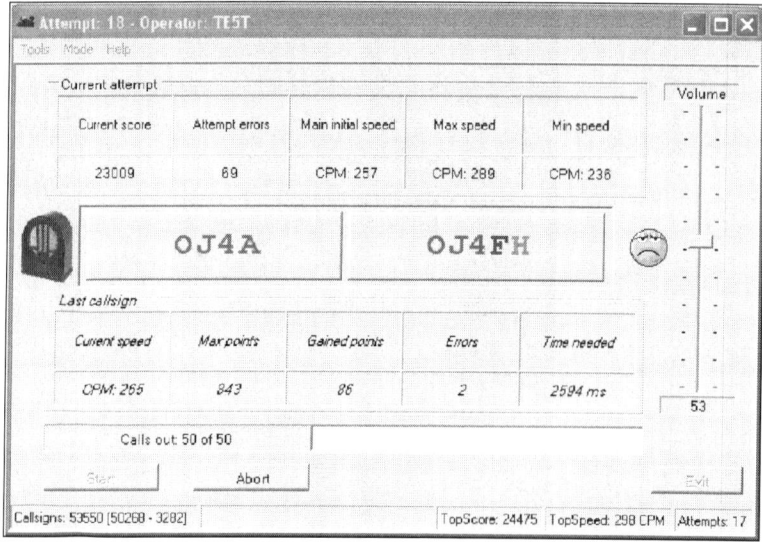

ARRL CW Practice
(www.arrl.org/code-practice-qst-source)

"Old Reliable." For years, the ARRL has been providing on-air sending alternately at 5, 7-1/2, 10, 13, and 15 wpm, and at 35, 30, 25, 20, 15, 13, and 10 wpm. The text is taken from *QST* magazine articles. Schedules and frequencies are available on the ARRL web site.

Your Next Decision

Naturally, you're going to need to *send* CW, as well as receive it, and that means making a basic decision. Should you be learning to send with a straight key or a paddle? A straight key is easy to use, quick to learn, and will allow you to proceed at a slow speed. Some people suggest learning with a straight key will also allow you to obtain a good feel for the length of a dit and a dah, and for word spacing, before moving to keying with a paddle. I prefer learning with a paddle. Do you really want to be poking along at 5 wpm, sending a letter at a time, when you should be learning to cruise along at a conversational 15 wpm?

A paddle allows faster, cleaner sending and it's easier on the wrist. It also creates dit/dah length *automatically*, so once you master using a paddle your sending should be easy copy. Even if you start with a straight key you're probably going to be moving, quickly, to a paddle for on-air QSOs, so why not start with one? (To use a paddle you'll need an external keyer or a rig that includes an internal keyer.) More on this and the various types of keys in Chapter 3.

VE3USP 's grandson uses a paddle to learn Morse code

Chapter 2

Getting Keyed Up

"As with the straight key, every bug operator sends differently. This introduces an individuality to the signal. It may be more musical or rhythmic than the code that comes out of a keyer. Some operators find this more interesting to listen to. It makes the signal stand out in a crowd." **– Brian, 9J2BO**

One of the important elements to sending good CW is using a good key, and one of the coolest things about operating CW is the variety of keys that you can use. Each type and model of key is unique. Like cars, some are very basic and some are high performance. Also, like car collectors, some hams have large key collections and love to regularly change the key that they "drive."

Illustration by W1CJD from *QST* May, 1934 (Copyright ARRL)

Semi-automatic keys, known as bugs, allow you to send a string of dits automatically. Paddles, used with a keyer, automate both the dits and the dahs. Of course, there's also the basic straight key. Each key has its own, unique feel and requires a different touch from its operator. It's really a very personal thing.

Like learning CW, mastering a key so that you're sending smooth and rhythmic CW can be a challenge, but once you've accomplished that you've opened the door to a symphony of fun.

Here are a few examples of the various instruments that you can use to make your own kind of CW music.

Straight Keys

This is the key that most people think of when they think of Morse code. It's simple and easy to use, but it's difficult and tiring to use it to send at a speed greater than 15 or 20 wpm. Some code instructors recommend that students begin with a straight key when they're learning to send, but others think that it's best to learn on the type of key that will allow you to eventually send at a "conversational speed" of greater than 20 wpm - i.e., a paddle.

Adjusting a Straight Key

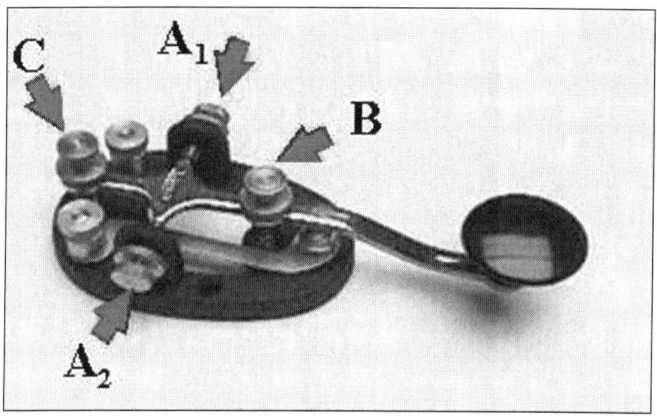

J38 Straight Key. N1FN Photo

CW aficionado Marshall, N1FN suggests these simple steps:

1. Unadjust the key. Loosen up everything and get to a common starting point, because each of the adjustments has some impact on the others. Loosen the spring tension on the arm (B) until no resistance is felt when you depress the knob. Open the contact spacing (C) as far as you can without removing the adjustment screw from the arm. Loosen the bearing tension screws (A) until the arm wobbles loosely.

2. Adjust the bearing tension. Choose one of the two bearings and tighten its adjustment screw (A) until you can just barely feel a bit of friction as you move the arm up and down. Now back off the screw until the arm just beings to move freely again; usually it's just a fraction of a degree of screw rotation, or about as fine an adjustment as you can make. Repeat with the other bearing tension adjustment screw. Setting the second bearing is likely to have had some effect on the first, so readjust the first bearing and then finally the second bearing. At this point the arm should move up and down freely with no sideways play, or "slop."

3. Adjust the contact spacing. The contact spacing determines the amount of vertical movement when you depress the arm. It's entirely a matter of taste, but if you haven't used a key before and haven't developed your own preferences, start with a sixteenth of an inch, or about the thickness of a penny. Adjust screw (C) until you have the desired spacing between the contacts.

4. Adjust the arm tension. Tighten the arm tension adjustment screw (B) to a comfortable level of tension on the arm. Again, this is a matter of preference, but a good rule of thumb is to set it for the *minimum* amount of pressure you need to feel that you are in control of the key.

Paddles

There are a wide variety of styles and sizes of paddles, but no matter which style you use they all have one thing in common: You touch one side of the paddle's finger pad(s) to send dits and the other to send dahs. The dits and dahs will continue as long as you keep pressure on the pad. For right handers, the left side is usually the dits and the right side is the dahs, but this can easily be reversed, if you prefer.

There are two types of paddles–the dual paddle (also known as Iambic) and the single paddle. With the Iambic paddle, which uses two finger pads, you're able to depress both pads simultaneously. This results in an alternating dit-dah until the pads are released. This feature allows an Iambic paddle to be used for an advanced keying technique known as *squeeze keying*. You cannot use a single pad paddle as a squeeze key. More about this technique shortly.

Many high-speed operators (40 wpm+) say they prefer the single paddle key, believing that a ham using it is less prone to make sending errors. Says Fabian, DJ1YFK, a member of the German high-speed CW team, "I switched from Iambic to a single lever key because I noticed that most mistakes I made at high speeds were caused by squeezing, especially additional dots and dashes at the end of a squeezed character like the period. Sending with a single lever key requires a little more mechanical effort, but for me the improved sending accuracy outweighs this drawback." (DJ1YFK is a nine-time winner of the German Cup for high-speed telegraphy.).

19

Different kinds of paddles use different methods for creating the amount of touch-pressure that you need to apply to a finger pad in order to trigger a dit or a dah. Some, such as the Bencher BY series, use a long, u-shaped adjustable spring to create that pressure. Others are spring-return paddles, which use a short spring attached to each finger pad. This allows a more precise pressure adjustment of each pad. "Hex," or "mag," style paddles use small magnets to do what the springs do. Each type of paddle has its own feel.

The process for adjusting paddles is similar to that for adjusting a straight key, but with more options. It's sort of like adjusting two straight keys placed on their sides and glued together. *Never* use sand paper or other highly abrasive substances to clean contacts on any paddle. Stick to running a piece of unlined paper gently between the contacts.

Adjusting The BY-style Paddle

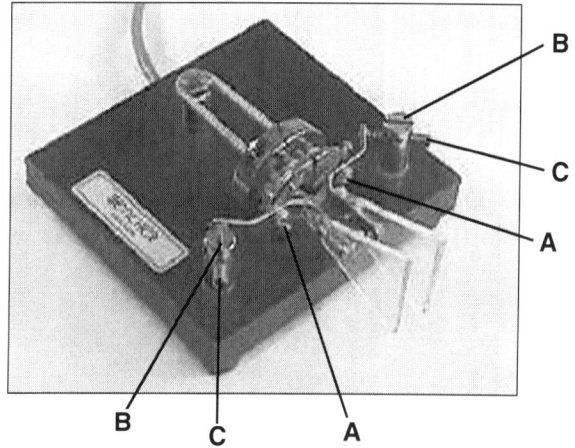

Bencher BY-1 Paddle. Vibroplex photo.

Adjust the finger pad pressure by either lengthening or shorten- ing the small screws (A) attached to each end of the spring. The lightest touch is achieved with the screws all the way in. To increase the touch, back out the screws.

Adjust the contact spacing by loosening the screws in the split posts (B) using a hex tool. Then turn the contact screws (C) to the desired spacing. Play with this until you achieve a feel that's com- fortable for you.

If you haven't used a paddle before, Marshall, N1FN suggests that you start with a contact spacing of about the thickness of a dime, or a bit less. The spacing doesn't have to be identical for each contact; in fact, many hams who also use a "bug" prefer a greater gap on the dah side.

Adjusting the Mag-style Paddle

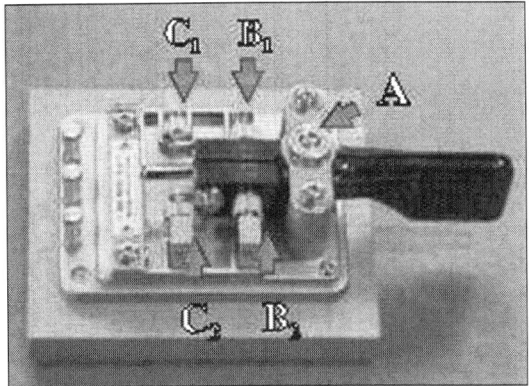

Mag-style Paddle. N1FN photo

Although the key looks a little different, the basic process is the same as it is for the BY-paddle. Screws (B) on each side adjust the tension of each lever arm. Tightening a screw increases the touch-pressure needed to send a dit or a dah. Loosening it decreases it. The contact screws (C) on each side adjust the spacing between the contacts. The information above about the size of the gap for the BY-1 also holds true for a mag paddle.

Some mag keys also allow adjustment of the bearing tension (A). If your paddle has this adjustment, tighten the screw (A) until you can just barely feel a bit of friction as you move the paddles back and forth. Then back off the screw until the paddles move freely again. Usually it's just a fraction of a degree of screw rotation, or about as fine an adjustment as you can make. The two levers should move from side to side freely, with no vertical play or "slop."

Some hex paddles require you to use a hex wrench or a screwdriver to adjust their settings. Generally speaking, more expensive paddles have finger screws with finely machined threads that can easily be adjusted, by hand, to precise settings.

Adjusting the Single Paddle

Again, the basic adjustments are the same. Use the side finger screws (A) to adjust the touch-pressure and (B) to adjust the contact gaps.

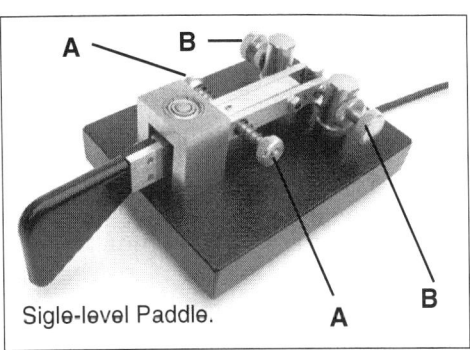

Sigle-level Paddle.

21

Keyers

A paddle that's not attached to an electronic keyer is like an electric guitar that's not plugged into an amp. You can't make music unless one is connected to the other.

The keyer is the piece of equipment that actually creates the dits and dahs electronically. (With a straight key or a bug the dit-dah creation is done mechanically.) Many modern ham rigs contain an internal keyer so that you only need to plug your paddle into the appropriate jack in the rig, make a menu selection about the type of keying that you want to use, and you're good to go.

MFJ-495
Keyer.

With most keyers you turn a knob to adjust the sending speed (some go as slow as 5 wpm and as fast as 60 wpm). You can also adjust the keying "weight," which is the dit to dah to space ratio. Increasing the weight a little, from the normal setting of 50%, slightly increases the length of the dits and dahs being sent. This may help slower CW (20 wpm or less) cut through band noise a little better. At higher speeds (35 wpm or more) some hams like to decrease the weight a bit.

Many keyers allow you to store several word-strings in memories. For example, you can store **CQ CQ CQ DE KR3E KR3E KR3E K** in a memory and just push a button on the keyer box, or an "F" key on your computer's keyboard, to send that. In another memory you can store **599 TU**. This can come in handy in a contest or a DX pileup.

If your rig doesn't have an internal keyer, or if you prefer the keying characteristics or the automated or memory functions of an external keyer, there are many to choose from. You can even build your own (see the August 1973 issue of *QST* magazine for an article about the WB4VVF Accu-Keyer).

Iambic Keying

Earlier in this chapter I mentioned "the *type* of keying."

With a dual paddle you can send characters by touching one side at a time *or* you can squeeze both sides together to repeatedly send **DI-DAH** or **DAH-DIT**. The way in which you begin and release that squeeze results in the character that's sent. You can use the squeeze method, also known Iambic keying, to send 7 letters (C Q R K Y F L) and a few numbers. There are two Iambic modes.

Mode A: Squeezing the paddles produces alternating dits and dahs until both paddles are released.

Mode B: Like Mode A, you squeeze both paddles to produce alternating dits and dahs. However, when the paddles are released, the keying continues to sending one more element i.e., a dit is sent if the paddles are released during a dah, or a dah is sent if the paddles are released during a dit.

Most keyers, whether internal or external, allow you to choose either mode.

Some hams swear by squeeze keying. They claim that it's more efficient...requiring fewer finger motions for some letters. However, many hams, particularly those who send at 40 wpm or faster, say that squeeze keying creates more sending errors than traditional keying. It can also be difficult to learn.

To understand what Iambic keying is all about, a video is better than a thousand words, and I recommend watching one that's available on YouTube, "Iambic Keyer and Technique," to get a real feel for this technique: https://youtu.be/ZdzjvIk_aY0.

Bugs

Many died-in-the-wool brass-pounders prefer to use semi-automatic keys known as "bugs." In fact, some have never used anything else. Virtually all bugs work the same way. When one side of the paddle is pressed, it triggers a pendulum arm with a contact that bounces against another contact to generate dots. The oscillation (and generation of dots) stops when the paddle is released. The speed of the oscillation is controlled by the position of the weight on the pendulum arm. The closer the weight is to the pivot point (the closer it is to you), the faster the pendulum will move and the faster you will be sending dits.

You press the other side of the paddle to create dahs, but they're not generated automatically. As with a straight key, pressing the paddle closes the contacts and releasing it opens it. Therefore, the length of each dah equals the length of time you press the paddle. Thus the term semi-automatic key.

Sending easy-to-copy CW with a bug, especially at faster speeds, requires a lot of skill and practice. It's also a lot more physically demanding on your wrist and arm than using a paddle.

Bug Adjustment

Even more than a paddle, a bug requires precise adjustment. Here's how to do it (with thanks to the U.S. Army Technical Manual, N1FN, WB8SIW, and WB6BEE):

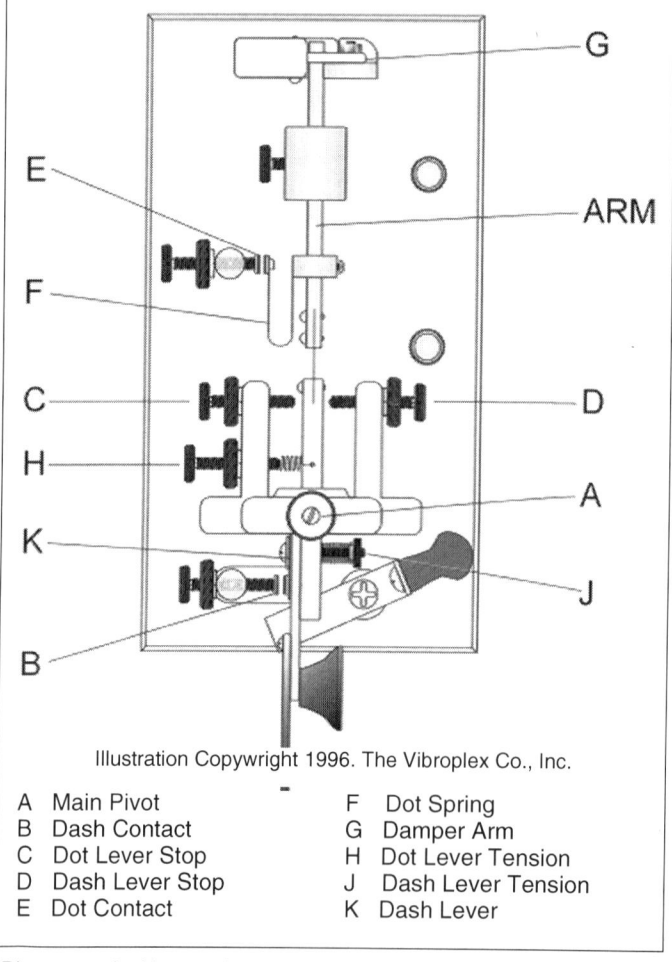

Illustration Copywright 1996. The Vibroplex Co., Inc.

A Main Pivot   F Dot Spring
B Dash Contact   G Damper Arm
C Dot Lever Stop   H Dot Lever Tension
D Dash Lever Stop   J Dash Lever Tension
E Dot Contact   K Dash Lever

Photo used with permisssion

1. Use the **Main Pivot** screw (**A**) to set the tension on the pendulum arm so that it moves freely from side to side, but with minimum vertical motion.

2. Adjust the **Dot Lever Stop** (**C**) so that the end of the pendulum arm rests *very gently* against the **Damper** (**G**). The pressure against the damper should be so light the arm does not push it away.

3. Adjust the **Dash Contact Screw** (**B**) so there is approximately 0.011 inch of space between the arm and the screw when the arm is at rest. (While 0.011 is recommended, up to 0.015 inch is acceptable.) Don't try to eyeball this. Use a feeler gauge to measure the gap. You can get one at most hardware or automotive stories and it will be well worth the price.

4. Adjust the **Dot Contact** (**E**) by pressing on the dot paddle and holding it in this position until the vibrating arm stops vibrating. While continuing to hold the dot paddle, adjust the dot contact screw so that the contact makes light, but solid contact with the **Dot Spring** (**F**). Don, WB6BEE has this suggestion: "Bring the dot contact (E) to the contact on the pendulum (F) until the contacts barely touch. Then tighten the dot contact screw (E) about a 1/4 twist. That adds a bit of weight to the dot, makes it a bit longer. If you back away the screw, it shortens the weight of the dot. You can hear both on the air, the machine gun dits and the dahs disguised as short dashes. There is a happy medium."

5. You can check the accuracy of your dit adjustment using a VOM. Connect the meter across the key's terminals and set it to the R x 1 position. Depress the dit paddle. A mid-scale deflection (typically between the 10- and 15-ohm range) should indicate correct dit adjustment.

6. Adjust the **Dot Retraction Spring** (**H**) and the **Dash Tension** (**J**) for the minimum tension necessary to ensure clean character formation.

7. If you're using multiple weights, move only one weight at a time along the arm to increase speed, leaving the unused weight(s) toward the rear of the arm (farthest away from you). Make sure the weights do not rub against the damper.

Some Useful Bug Stuff

- Again, as mentioned earlier in this chapter, *never* use sand paper or other highly abrasive substances to clean contacts. Stick to running a piece of unlined paper gently between the contacts.

- Unlike a paddle, the bug is manipulated mainly by rolling the wrist and forearm, as opposed to moving the fingers. Make sure you have a reasonably flat surface on which you can rest your forearm, just as you would when using a standard straight key.
- Don't try to keep up with the other guy who's cruising along at 30 wpm on a paddle. It's a rare bug operator who can sustain good CW at higher speeds.
- A re-usable adhesive, such as Blue-Tack®, works well on the feet of a bug to keep it from moving around your operating desk. You can also use a mouse pad. (You shouldn't need this for most paddles. If a paddle moves you're probably slapping it too hard.)
- There are many different kinds of bugs. Wouldn't it be nice if you could "test drive" a few before you shell out a lot of bucks to buy one? You can if you're a member of the Straight Key Century Club. SKCC (www. skccgroup.com) has a straight key lending library from which members can borrow!

"How-To" CW Videos on YouTube

A number of hams have gone to the trouble of making videos to share their process for adjusting their keys or for sending properly. Here are some that I've found on YouTube:

"How to Adjust a Vibroplex Bug" by WB8SIW:
   http://youtu.be/qekmyx31Uxw

"How to Operate a Straight Key" by ghdkey (in Japanese with English sub-titles):
   http://youtu.be/ncOcgarGJHI

"U.S. Navy "Morse Code Radio Operator Training," 1944 (a real oldie-but-goodie):
   https://www.youtube.com/watch?v=iC5RQNSSZH0

Keyboards

There are times when you may want to swap your key for a computer keyboard. During CW contests, when you are spending hours just sending a short contest exchange of a signal report and serial number (e.g., **N9RV 599 007**), it's much easier to do this, and far less tiring, by hitting a PF key on your keyboard than by sending this with a key. There are also hams who prefer to use a keyboard because they have a physical ailment, such as arthritis, that prevents them from sending clean CW with a key.

If you're already using your keyboard with a computer logging program that interacts with your rig, it's easy to also use it to send CW. If you don't have a direct computer-rig interface, many keyers that you use with a paddle also allow a keyboard to be connected.

Key Collections

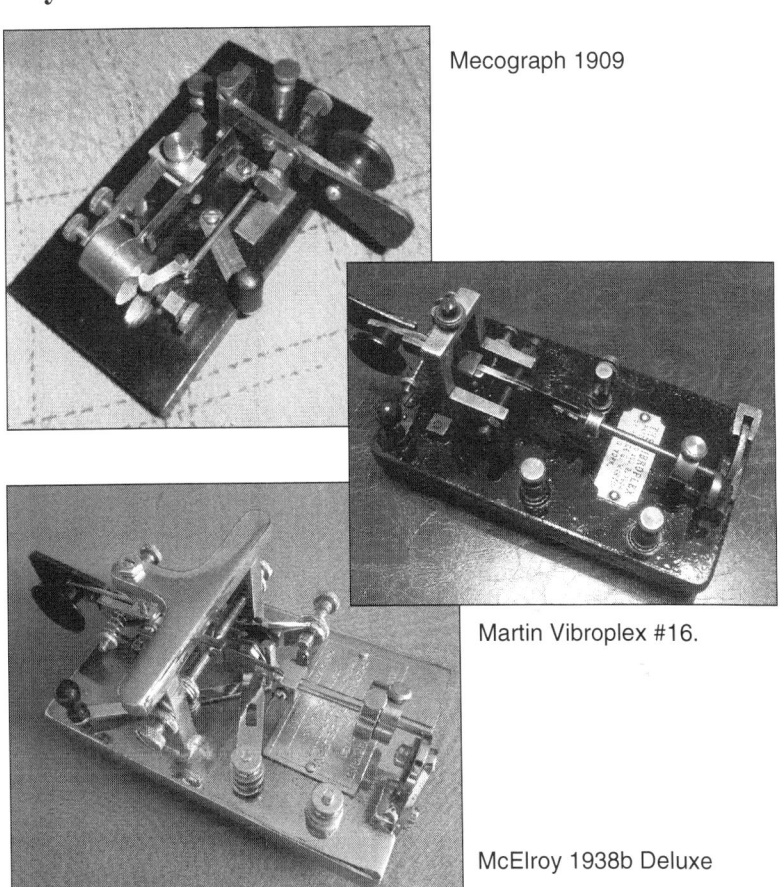

Mecograph 1909

Martin Vibroplex #16.

McElroy 1938b Deluxe

Fabio, IKØIXI has enough bugs and straight keys in his collection so that, if he likes, he can use a different key each week of the year. Fabio's oldest key is a Martin Vibroplex, serial number 16, which was made in 1904, the first year of production. His rarest is a 1909 Mecograph, and his favorite is his McElroy 1938B DeLuxe. You can see Fabio's great collection at: nuke.ik0ixi.it (click on Morse Keys Collection).

27

Here are the web sites of a few more serious key collectors:

G3YUH Key collection: **www.g3yuh.com**

I6QON Station & Keys: **www.i6qon.jimdo.com**

K5BCQ Collection (many are home-brew):
www.qsl.net/k5bcq/KEYS/KEYS.html

N3CW Paddle Museum: **http://qsl.net/n3cw/paddles/index.html**

NØUF's Key Collection: **http://qsl.net/n0uf/keys.htm**

PA3EGH Key Collection: **http://www.pa3egh.nl/morsekeys.html**

Chapter 3

On The Air

"When I operate SSB my wife says I'm 'cheating'....She says ham radio is 'diddy-dahdah'; SSB is just another cordless phone."–**K2TA** (Tnx: **K3WWP**)

Calling CQ

You've been working hard on your CW skills and now it's time to take the plunge and make that first QSO.

You tune across the CW portion of 40 meters and wow! The stations are going so fast! But, let's jump in and try a CQ at a speed at which you're comfortable operating. A considerate operator should answer your CQ at the speed at which you send it. Ready?

But wait! Before you begin sending your CQ, check to see if the frequency that you want to use is clear. Send: **QRL?** (Is the frequency in use?). It's possible that a QSO may be in progress, even if you don't hear it. Due to propagation, you may not be hearing the station that is sending, but the other station in that QSO may be hearing you loud and clear. Listen for four or five seconds and then send **QRL?** again. If you hear a response of **QRL** (the frequency IS in use), **C** (yes), or anything similar, move to another frequency and repeat the process.

Now, knowing you have a clear frequency, you're ready to call "CQ". You're going to be using several pro-signs and procedural signals during this process. If you're unfamiliar with some of these, there's a complete list later in this chapter.

Rule number 1: The most important part of the CQ is *your call.* Resist the temptation to call "CQ" a dozen times followed by your call only once or twice. The sound of "CQ" is easily recognizable to a station tuning the band, but your call is not, so emphasize your call and send your CQ in a predictable pattern. This will give the receiving station a few opportunities to copy your call even if he misses part of it due to QSB, QRM, QRN, etc.

The ARRL recommends a 3x3 pattern: **CQ CQ CQ DE KA1XXX KA1XXX KA1XXX K,** pausing for 10 or 20 seconds to listen for a response and, if nothing is heard, repeating the 3x3 pattern until someone responds.

I like to use a 3x3 CQ followed by a 2x2 and a 1x1. For example:

CQ CQ CQ DE KA1XXX KA1XXX KA1XXX

CQ CQ DE KA1XXX KA1XXX

CQ DE KA1XXX K

You'll hear a variety of CQ patterns, but the important things to remember are: 1) Your call is the most important thing that you're sending and 2) keep the whole thing short enough so that a station that hears you doesn't get bored waiting for you to finish and tune away.

The length of your CQ, and the pattern, also depends on the band conditions and the speed at which you're sending.

At 27 or 28 wpm I'm likely to use a 3x3, 2x2, 1x1 pattern. If I'm sending slowly, I'll probably use the 3x3 recommended by the ARRL. If I'm CQing on 6 meters, where the QSB may be very fast with signals appearing only in short bursts, I may use only a single 2x2 or even a 1x2 pattern, **CQ DE KA1XXX KA1XXX K**, even if my speed is relatively fast.

Before too long you'll have the thrill of hearing another station answering your CQ: **KA1XXX de KR3E KR3E AR**

Note that the answering station should have sent his call two or three times but your call only once. That's because the other person assumes that you will recognize the sound of your own call, so there's really no need for him to repeat it. On the other hand, that station should also realize that he will be a stranger to you and that you may have trouble copying his call, so he repeats it two or three times. (Be prepared that some stations do not send your call at all, only sending their own, when responding to your CQ. I don't recommend this, but unfortunately it's become a common practice, so be ready for it.)

What if that station finishes calling you and you're still not sure of his call letters? Simple: The Q-signal **QRZ?** ("Who is calling me?") was designed just for this. (A full list of Q-signals can be found in Chapter 4). A simple **QRZ? DE KA1XXX** should result in the station sending his call again, hopefully two or three times.

Answering a CQ

If you're answering someone's CQ, the first thing to do is to be sure you're transmitting as close as you can to the calling station's

30

frequency. This is called "spotting" or "zero-beating." Your object is to have the tone that you hear when you're transmitting (the "side-tone") match the tone that you hear when you're listening to the other guy. When they match you're zero-beat. You may even hear a sort of pulsing, beating sound when the two tones cancel each other out, hence the term "zero-beat."

Your rig should have a "spot" button that, when you push it, will let you hear your side-tone without actually transmitting. Push the button, listen to the side-tone, and tune your receiver until the tone of the sending station matches your side-tone. (My K-3 has a really neat feature that allows you to automatically zero-beat a station just by pushing two buttons, but I still like to tweak it myself by twisting the dial to match the tones. The manual for your rig should guide you through this if you need help.)

The whole process should only take a couple of seconds, and once you're done, you're ready to give the other station a call. Remember what I said earlier: Send his call once so he knows, for sure, he is the station that you're calling. Then send your call twice.

KR3E DE KA1XXX KA1XXX $\overline{\text{AR}}$

If he has trouble copying, he might send **QRZ?** or he might send **AGN** (again) or even just **?**

If the station is able to copy part of your call he might send **KA1?** or **1** or whatever part he copied.

There's no need to waste time sending his call again. Just send yours once. If he asks you for another repeat, send your call twice. Sometimes slowing down just a bit helps. Before too long either he'll have you in his log or he'll decide that he just can't copy you well enough and he'll return to CQing.

Time to Chat

OK, you've made a contact. What next? It's simple because, just as on SSB, most CW QSOs begin by following the basic format of signal report (RST) followed by location (QTH) and name. Also, to keep things brief, standard CW abbreviations are used. (See Chapter 4 for a list.) For example:

KR3E DE KA1XXX GE OM ES TNX FOR THE CALL $\overline{\text{BT}}$ UR RST 579 $\overline{\text{BT}}$ QTH BOSTON MA $\overline{\text{BT}}$ NAME JOHN BT HW? KR3E DE KA1XXX K

"Good evening old man and thanks for the call. –Break– Your signal report is 579 –Break– My location is Boston, Mass –Break– My name is John –Break– How do you copy me?"

There will be variations of this, of course. Some stations use the BT pro-sign to separate parts of their transmission and others use punctuation marks. Some may choose not to use RST and QTH, and instead send something a bit shorter, such as: **UR 579 HR IN BOSTON,** but the general format will be the same.

Although many stations send each item (RST, QTH, name) twice, if signals are strong there's probably no need to send it more than once...unless your name or QTH is unusual. If the other station misses something, he can easily ask you to repeat it: **PSE RPT UR NAME** or **UR NAME AGN PSE** or just **UR NAME?**

Once you've sent your information, the other station will respond with his signal report to you, his location, and his name. He may move on to tell you about his rig and antenna, and maybe the weather, or he may leave it to you to begin that part of your QSO.

This is enough information (probably more than enough, you may think) for your first CW QSO. When you're more comfortable using CW, and particularly as your skill and speed improve, there are unlimited topics to discuss. If you don't recognize the other ham's location, ask him about it. You can mention your profession and ask about his. Doing this I've met a Grammy Award-winning gospel singer and the electric bass player from a well-known fusion jazz group; a retired Texas Ranger (police, not baseball) and a Texas rancher; a retired commander of a nuclear submarine; the president of news for a major TV/radio network; and a pediatrician in Japan who plays the cello. If your cat jumps on your operating desk, you can mention that, too. Maybe the other operator has three cats!

There's a lot more to a QSO than just the basics but U.S. hams need to remember that no commercial/business can be conducted on the air.

QRU?

At some point, of course, the band will fade, your fist will grow tired, or you will just plain run out of things to say. Many stations, however, seem to have trouble saying a simple "goodbye." They tend to drag things out, rambling on with all sorts of pleasantries. Really, all that's needed to wrap things up is a simple:

NW QRU HR OM $\overline{BT}$ TNX QSO ES HPE C U AGAIN $\overline{BT}$ 73 $\overline{SK}$ KR3E DE KA1XXX K

"Now nothing further here old man. Thanks for the contact and hope to see you again. Best wishes. End of contact. KR3E from KA1XXX. Over."

Note that I did not send "73s" or "best 73." The signal "73" means "best wishes." It doesn't make sense to send "best wishess" or "best best wishes," does it?

Places to Hang Out on the Air

Although there are no longer any Novice bands, band segments where beginners were forced to hang out with other beginners, there are some frequencies where you're likely to find slower CW operators and Elmers, those more experienced hams who will offer to help. The FISTS CW club includes a significant number of members who are relatively new to CW and who operate at slower speeds. Also, members of the Straight Key Century Club (SKCC) operate at relatively slower speeds because of the speed limitations of their straight keys and bugs. SKCC even has a frequency devoted to Elmering new CW operators (7.114 MHz). The club calls it "a safe haven for CW newcomers to get on the air."

Each of these clubs has suggested operating frequencies on every band:

FISTS: 1.808, 3.558, 7.058 and 7.028, 10.118, 14.058, 18.085, 21.058, 24.908, 28.058, 50.058, 144.058

SKCC: 1.820, 3.530, 3.550 primary, 7.055 primary, 7.120, 10.120, 14.050, 14.114, 18.080, 21.050, 21.114, 24.910, 28.050, 28.114, 50.090, 144.070

No matter where you're operating on the band, a courteous CW operator should respond to a CQ at the speed at which it's sent. The reverse is also true. If you're answering a 15 wpm CQ at 10 wpm the other station *should* slow down to your 10 wpm speed. If he doesn't, there's no shame in sending **PSE QRS** ("please slow down"). However, it's better not to call a station that is sending significantly faster than your copying ability. He or she is sending at that speed because that's the speed at which he or she wants to hold a conversation. Asking for a significant slow-down just isn't cool.

Traffic Nets

We're not talking about bumper-to-bumper cars here. In ham radio lingo "traffic" refers to messages that are sent using a standard format, very much like a telegram. In most cases, these messages contain only short "hello," or birthday messages and greetings to friends. In an emergency, however, these radiograms can contain urgent and sometimes lifesaving information. Participating in a CW traffic net is a great way to improve your sending and

ARRL Radiogram form

copying skills and to learn on-air discipline. One day, too, you might be called upon to put these skills to the test in an emergency.

Don't worry about not being able to send or receive fast enough as you begin. Almost every state has a beginners' traffic net, usually called a "slow speed net." My friend Milt, K4OSO had a great experience with the slow net in Maryland:

"One particular activity that improved my confidence and ability to handle most situations was learning traffic handling on the Maryland Slow Net. Net speed was maximum 10 wpm (and flexible); the instructors were patient and considerate. That training gave me the confidence I desperately needed. I'm now an Instructor/NCS on that net and watch the transformation of new ops from tentative and unsure to ops who would be welcomed on an NTS (National Traffic System high speed) traffic net throughout the country. It's easy and painless and proceeds at the new op's own pace. Even if you don't become an active traffic handler, the training is invaluable for learning general operating practices."

KV5R has created an excellent six-lesson, on-line course for hams who would like to become involved in traffic handling. You can find it at: http://texastrafficnet.org/training.asp

Chapter 7 of the *ARRL Operating Manual* also provides a good introduction to traffic handling.

You can search for a traffic net in your state at: http://www.arrl.org/arrl-net-directory-search

Contests and Other Events

Operating in a contest is an excellent way to improve your CW speed, while also possibly working some new states, counties, or DX entities. However, be careful which event you select for your first few forays into contesting. Jumping into the wrong "test" would be like trying to drive a bicycle on a California freeway.

One thing about all contests that makes it easier for a new CW operator to participate is that, with small variations, they all follow a basic format. Each station exchanges certain information, which must be logged and submitted with the contest entry. Often this information consists of a signal report plus a consecutive serial number. (The signal report is traditionally given as 599 no matter what the station's actual signal strength is). Thus, a contest exchange is typically this:

CQ TEST K9UIY TEST (These CQs are usually short 1x1s and the **DE** before the call is often left out. Many contest stations substitute "TEST" for "K" to signal that they are standing by for a call in a contest)

KR3E (In a contest an answering station sends only its own call)

KR3E 599 001 (KR3E is K9UIY's first contact)

R 599 013 (K9UIY is KR3E's 13th contact. "TU" or "CFM" may sometimes be used instead of "R")

TU K9UIY TEST (The "TU" acknowledges that the exchange was received)

I would recommend *not* using a keyboard, or sending with a memory programmed in, when you first begin to operate in contests. Use the contest as an opportunity to improve your sending skill by sending by hand as well as improving your skill at copying.

Most contesters dash off their exchanges at a high speed, usually in the 28–30 wpm range. There are some contests that run at a more relaxed pace, however, and they're a good place to stick your paddle into the contesting waters without getting swamped by the wakes of all of those motorboats zooming by in other contests.

State QSO parties usually run at a slower pace than most other contests, with some stations taking time to say hello, or even have a very brief chat if they run into an old friend. These are also good places to work on your Worked All States or USA-CA Counties

Awards, and there's a state QSO party almost every weekend. The exchange in most state parties is signal report plus your county or state.

The FISTS CW Club holds a "get your feet wet" activity once a month for club members and it's another good way to ease into contesting. It's held on the third Sunday of every month from 0001 UTC to 2400 UTC on 80 and 40 meters. Look for activity around 3.558 and 7.110 MHz. Exchange: Name, QTH, FISTS#, RST. More info at: www.fistsna.org/operating.html#feetwet.

The CW Operators Club has a contest that runs for one hour, during each of three start times, every Wednesday (U.S. time). Occasionally they devote one Wednesday to new operators and ask all contestants to slow to 20 wpm or slower. Listen for stations calling **CQ CWT** during these events. You can get more information on these mini-contests at: http://cwops.org/cwt.html.

A contest calendar can be found in various ham publications, and also on WA7BNM's contest calendar web site: www.hornucopia.com/contestcal/weeklycont.php.

If you think you're ready to enter the contesting world, here are some tips from award-winning contester Pat, N9RV. While these can apply to SSB as well as to CW, take particular note of the first tip:

• Learn CW. It's a lot easier to make a respectable contest score from a smaller station on CW. There are lots of SSB-only operators who were motivated to learn CW so that they could operate CW contests. Strive to be one of them.

• Don't be a loner. It really helps in getting started if you have access to contesters who you can talk to and trade experiences with. Not just "Field Day" contesters who only get on in June, but other contesters who put in efforts around the year.

• Be careful who you learn from. Like anything else in life, there are good examples to follow and there are bad ones. Strive to be more like the better scoring operators; listen to what they do and how they do it. Even if what they do is light years away from where your skills are today, it will help you tremendously.

• Spend some time at it. It's hard to acquire basic operating skills if you never operate. Contests have a faster pace than other operating QSOs and events, and getting the confidence and experience to get through quickly or react quickly to those calling you doesn't come any other way.

At the higher levels of contesting, where every second counts as contestants try to put as many stations into the log as possible, some stations try to shave a few milli-seconds off each contest exchange by shortening the dits and dahs in each number. For example, the number nine, which is normally sent as **DAH-DAH-DAH-DAH-DIT**, would be sent as **DAH-DIT**. The number five, **DI-DI-DI-DI-DIT**, becomes simply **DIT**. You've probably heard some of this in a regular QSO when a signal report of 599 is sent as 59N or 5NN.

These abbreviations are called "cut numbers." The most common are:

1 – **DI-DAH**

5 – **DIT**

9 – **DAH-DIT**

∅ – **DAH-DAH-DAH** or **DAH**

Off-Air Contests

Not all contesting is done on the air. Some major ham radio conventions include a pileup contest where contestants listen to a recording of a simulated pileup as if they were the DX station. The winner is the person with the most correct calls written down.

For the cream of the high-speed CW crop, the International Amateur Radio Union (IARU) holds an annual High Speed Telegraphy World Championship at speeds exceeding 120 wpm.

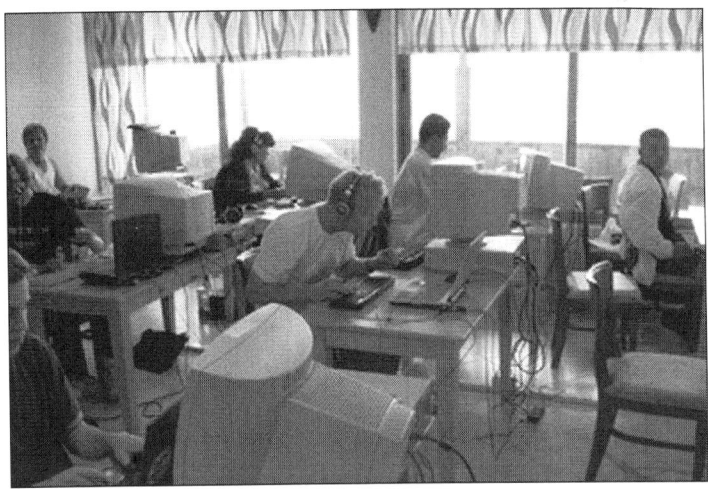

Operators copying CW in an international high speed championship.

Individuals and teams compete in four events: a pileup, receiving individual callsigns, receiving random text, and sending random text. The current world records for callsign copying are 194 wpm for an OM, held by EW8GS, and 180 wpm for a YL, held by LZ2CWW. Wow! For a taste of what the callsign event contest is like download the free RufzXP software at www.rufzxp.net and try copying various speeds.

DXing

I have just under 300 DXCC entities confirmed. They include KP1, YVØ, SV/A, VP8G, 3Y/P, KH3, VU7, and KH7K.

In my 50-plus years on the air I have never had a tower. I have never had a directional antenna. I have never run more than 100 watts output.

I could never have come even *close* to working this much DX with my simple setup if I had not used CW. CW is the DXer's friend.

You get a lot more bang-for-the-buck with a CW signal. In a noisy environment, QRN, QSB or poor band conditions a weak CW tone is much easier for the brain to de-code than a weak voice transmission. On the air, a CW signal can have a 10 to 20 dB advantage over SSB. It may take you a little longer than the guys with the "big guns," but with CW and just a modest setup if you can hear 'em you can almost always work 'em.

Nigel, G3TXF operates as ZD9XF from Tristan da Cunha.

Some DX stations welcome a nice rag-chew with you but others want no more than a quick exchange of signal reports and, perhaps, name and QTH. Let the DX station take the lead. If you call and he responds with a signal report, his name and his QTH, he'd probably like to at least exchange that information and probably rig and weather as well. If it appears that the DX operator speaks a bit of English you might try to have a little longer conversation. On the other hand, if his response is simply **<your call> 599** then it's likely that he wants a similar response from you, i.e., **R 599 TU**, and no more.

If the station is in a relatively rare location, or has an unusual prefix or something else that makes him sought-after, you're probably going to have to compete with other stations who want him in their log. Now you're calling in a pileup and the fun begins!

Here's what I've learned over the years, with some added suggestions from DXpeditioners G3SXW, G3RWF, ON4UN, and ON4WW.

Start by listening. Don't just jump in and begin calling willy-nilly. Whether the DX station is listening for calls on his own frequency ("working simplex") or transmitting on one frequency and listening on another ("working split"), there should be some sort of pattern to his operating. Does the DX send **TU** to signal that he's ready for the next call? Is his call the final thing that he sends? Is he sending **UP**? All good DX operators have a pattern and it's worthwhile to take time to discover it by listening.

Never click on a DX Cluster spot to automatically QSY to the DX station's frequency and immediately begin calling. Why? Re-read the "Start by listening" paragraph in this chapter.

Call *only* when the DX is not transmitting. The best way to ensure that you're not "doubling" with him is to use full break-in when you transmit so that you can listen even while you're transmitting. (See Operating QSK later on in this chapter.)

Send your call once and then *listen* for a second or so. This is particularly important if you're not operating full break-in. You need to be able to hear the DX when he responds, so take a second to do that.

If the DX is operating "simplex," with dozens of other stations calling smack on his frequency, use your rig's XIT control to QSY so that you're calling 10 or 15 Hz above the DX's frequency. Your tone will be slightly different from that of all those other stations and that difference may help your call stand out from the crowd.

Sending slightly slower than the rest of the pileup may also help you stand out from the others. (A slower speed may also be easier to copy in poor band conditions.) Resist the temptation to send faster than the DX.

Timing can be crucial. Says Roger, G3SXW: "If I'm picking up callers on their first call, then throw your call in right away. But if I'm struggling, then try to delay sending by 2–3 seconds. Your call might be in the clear when the others all have stopped sending."

If the DX is operating "split," then that DX station should be sending **UP** (and less frequently **DN**) indicating that he is listening above (or below) his transmitting frequency. Many DX stations will send **UP1** or **UP2** indicating that they're starting to listen 1 or 2 kHz up from where they're sending. In order to work a station operating split, you need to listen to the DX's frequency but transmit within his listening "window." Taking time to determine where that is before you begin to call will pay dividends.

When working "split," many DX stations tune from low to high, picking out calls, so if you can call just a bit higher than the last station that was worked you may be next in line. Except in the largest pileups, which may be spread across as much as 15 or 20 kHz, most DX stations will sweep 5 to 7 kHz and then return to their starting point to begin their upward listening again. I've had some success calling a few Hz below the DX station's starting point, which is usually pretty clear of other callers.

It's not unusual for a DX station to make a directional call, e.g., **TZ6BB UP 1 NA**. The "NA" indicates that TZ6BB wants calls *only* from stations in North America. Sending SA means South America, EU is Europe, JA usually means anywhere in Asia. You get the idea. If the DX says he wants EU calls and you're not in EU do not call.

The same holds true if the DX responds by sending something like **W8?** or **3E?**. That means he has copied part of a call and wants everyone else to QRX while he completes the call. Only someone with W8 or 3E in their call should reply. Everyone else QRX!

If the DX copies your call correctly, do *not* send it again when you respond and send your report. *Do* repeat it if he copies your call incorrectly. When I have to repeat my call I send **DE KR3E**. The **DE** serves as an indicator to the DX that my correct call will follow.

It should go without saying, but make sure that you can actually *hear* the DX before you call. You can't work him if you can't hear him, but it's amazing how many stations try anyway.

Excellent and detailed information about working DX can be found on the web site of DX University (www.dx-code.org). Among the things that you'll find there is a DX Code of Conduct, which was developed by an international group of DXers. For your convenience, and because its recommendations are so important to skilled and ethical DXing, a copy is included at the end of this book.

Operating QSK

The pro-sign **QSK?** asks, "can you operate full break-in?" In other words, can you listen to what's happening on your frequency at the same time as you're transmitting. If your rig allows you to do it, it's a very good thing to do.

There are actually two modes of QSK: Full break-in and semi break-in and most rigs have both.

Semi break-in automatically switches from transmit to receive a second or so after you stop sending and then goes back into transmit when you start to send again. It's CW's version of VOX (automatic voice control). Most rigs allow you to adjust the length of the break-in delay.

Full break-in is really great, but it takes some getting used to. The switching between transmit and receive is so quick that it occurs between each character that you send, even at high speed. On a good rig this switching is done so seamlessly that it seems as if you're *always* listening to your frequency as you're sending.

If you're rag chewing, using full break-in allows the other station to break into your sending to tell you, for example, that your signal has dropped down into the noise or that he needs to step away for a phone call. It also allows you to hear if QRM pops up on top of you, giving you the opportunity to QRX until the QRMing station stops sending.

In contesting, using full break-in is a big help. In a DX pileup it's so necessary that it should be a law! When you're calling the same station as dozens, or even hundreds, of others are calling, you need to be able to listen to the DX station while *you're* sending so that you can hear the moment that *he* begins sending someone's call. You don't want to be transmitting, with your receiver silenced, when the DX station sends your call and you shouldn't continue to send after he sends the call of someone else.

Best of all, once you master copying CW in your mind, and you're holding QSOs at 20 wpm or faster, you'll find that two stations using full QSK can hold a real, conversation-style conversation…interrupting each other in the middle of a transmission, or a sentence, with a thought that just occurred. There's no need to wait until the other guy stops transmitting and turns it back over to you. Just go ahead and start sending. He'll hear you and will stop to let you continue. He can do the same when you're sending. Just like a real chat!

CW Filters

Many times a crowded band or QRN makes copy difficult. That's when it's really nice to have a couple of filters in your rig.

Using a filter is like cropping a picture of a group of people. If you don't crop it at all, you'll have a picture of the whole bunch, but the tighter you crop it, the fewer people you'll see. On the air, a wide filter will give you a broad "view" of your surroundings on the band. A narrow filter will cut out the stations you don't want in your "picture" and focus in on the one that you do want.

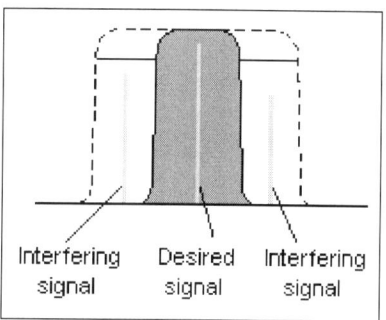

A CW filter limits the bandwidth to what you want to hear.

Older rigs generally have a few filters with fixed widths. Most newer rigs include filters whose widths can be adjusted, incrementally, from wide (for SSB and even for AM listening) to narrow (best for CW). You're going to want to use different widths for different situations.

On CW, I generally set my filter around 550 or 600 Hz when I call CQ so that I can hear a station calling me even if he's a little off frequency. Before I call CQ, I set it a bit wider so that when I send **QRL?** I can hear if there are any stations operating nearby. If they have only a wide filter (e.g., 1.5 kHz) in their rig, I may interfere with them even though I'm operating 500 Hz away, and I may look for a clearer spot to call my CQ.

Once I begin my rag-chew, if there is only a little QRM and/or QRN, I may leave the filter set around 550 Hz, or even widen it a bit, because a slight widening will improve the fidelity, or "sound," of the signal in my headset. If there *is* some kind of interference, however, I'll narrow the filter as much as necessary to make the signal easier to copy.

If I'm operating in a contest, where signals are packed right on top of each other, I usually reduce my filter width to 250 or 300 Hz so that I can separate the signals as much as possible. Some avid contesters who want to be as selective as possible even use a 150 Hz filter.

Reverse Beacon Network

One of the advantages of working CW is that you can take advantage of a neat tool called the Reverse Beacon Network (RBN). RBN is a web-based feed that allows you to see which other CW stations are on the air, and on what frequencies, at that moment worldwide. It's a great way to see what bands are open to your part of the world and where your own signal is being heard.

Unlike a traditional DX cluster, many of which depend solely on CW operators inputting "spots" of the stations they've heard, the RBN uses a worldwide network of more than 100 hams who dedicate receivers and antennas to monitoring the bands, 160m–6m. These receiving setups skim the bands and then post the calls of all of the CW stations that they find calling CQ. These calls then appear, in real time, on www.reversebeacon.net.

The screen-grab below shows, among the many spots:

- UA4UAR is on 3.522.5, sending at 25 wpm and heard by the skimmers at DJ2BC, SV8RV and IK3STG.

- EI5DS is on 5.355.5, sending at 23 wpm ad heard by the skimmer at DL6ZB.

- PA3CWN is on 7.010, sending at 24 wpm and heard by the skimmer at ON4KC and others.

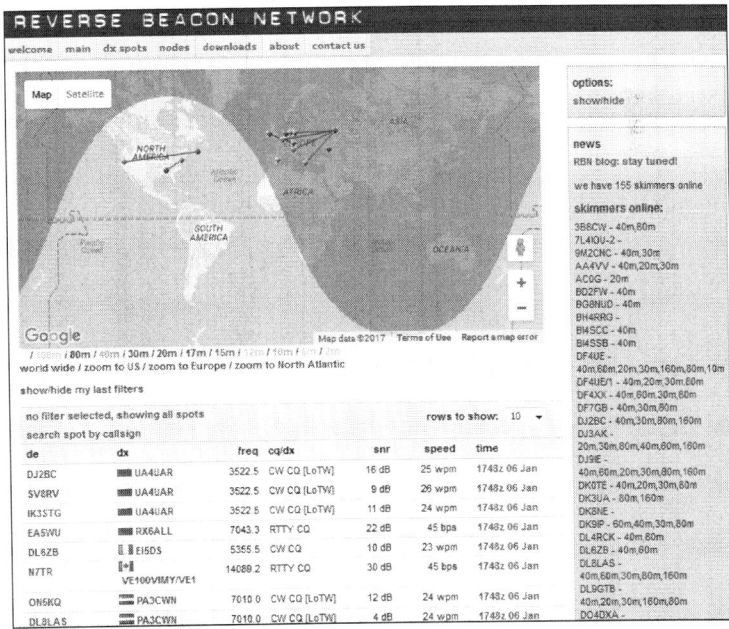

Reverse Beacon Network.

You should be able to see your own call pop up if you call CQ a few times and then watch the RBN feed. The RBN web site says that on an average day the service pumps out more than 120 spots per minute and during a contest the flow can average 20 per second!

In addition to appearing on the RBN web site, these skimmed calls are also fed to many of the traditional DX Telnet cluster nodes, including ARCluster Version 6 and CC Cluster. (Each of those two nodes gives its users the opportunity to select whether or not to include RBN calls, along with the traditional spots, in what they receive.) You can find a list of Telnet cluster nodes that use the RBN at: www.dxcluster.info.

There's a lot more to learn about the RBN and its various features and filters. It's all available at: www.reversebeacon.net.

Chapter 4

Signs, Signals, and Procedures

If uv evr sent a txt msg with lil words u know hw to send short cw.

Short Stuff

CW operators use a lot of abbreviations on the air, making it possible to squeeze a lot of information into a short amount of time. The abbreviations also serve as a common ham language, allowing hams from around the world to hold simple conversations regardless of their native tongue.

Most of these abbreviations are common-sense condensations of larger words, but some, such as "c" (which sounds like the Spanish "si"), may have their roots in other languages. Here are a few of the more common abbreviations that you may hear:

abt = about
adr - address
agn = again (sometimes used to ask for a repeat)
ant = antenna
arnd = around
b4 = before
bk = break (used to quickly turn it over to the other station without sending callsigns. Also used to "break" into a QSO)
buro – bureau (as in "QSL via the bureau")
c = yes (like the Spanish "si")
cfm: confirm
ck = check (the word-count in a formal message; see Chapter 2 about traffic nets)
clg = calling
cndx = conditions, as in "band conditions"
cple = couple
cpy = copy

cud = could

cul = see you later

cuz = because

de = from

dr = dear (commonly used as a sign of respect before a name)

ere = here

es = and

evr = ever

fb = fine business

fer = for

fm = from

fwd = forward

ga = good afternoon

gd = good day

ge = good evening

gg = good going

gl = good luck

gn = good night

gnd = ground

gud = good

hi = the sound of laughter (sometimes the "h" is extended with extra dits to indicate a lot of laughing)

hny – happy new year

hr = here, hear, or hour

hw = how

lil = little

lsn = listen

msg = message

mx = merry christmas

nw = now

ob = old boy

oc = old chap

om = old man

ot = old timer

rcvr = receiver

tdy = today

tt = that

tmw = tomorrow

tnx or tks = thanks

test = testing or short for contest, e.g., "CQ test"

u = you

uv: you've

wx = weather

xmtr = transmitter

yr = year
ystdy = yesterday
73 = best wishes
88 = love and kisses

Pro-signs

These are instructional signals that are made up of two or three letters sent with no spacing between them. They sound like one character, not two or three, and in print they're written with an overscore mark above them.

$\overline{AR}$ = End of a transmission. $\overline{AR}$ is used after calling a station with which contact has not already been established. It is also used at the end of a formal radiogram message. Although it isn't intended to be used this way, some stations use it at the end of every transmission.

$\overline{AS}$ = Wait, stand by for a short time.

$\overline{BT}$ = This is used to separate conversation topics in a QSO. Sending several in a row can serve as a "place holder," while you think of what you want to say next. In a formal radiogram it's a separation, or break, between the address and the text and between the text and the signature.

$\overline{IMI}$ = This is a standard CW question mark, but it also can be used to ask for a repeat of difficult words. Frequently this pro-sign is also being used (although it shouldn't be) as a substitute for "QRZ?"

$\overline{SK}$ = The communication is concluded or clear. The ARRL recommends sending this before the final station identification (e.g., **73 ES GL $\overline{SK}$ W1DV DE KR3E**). Many stations seem to now send this *after* the final ID, rather than before it. Sent either way, the message is the same.

$\overline{HH}$ = A series of dits indicates you have made a mistake. You don't have to be careful about how many dits you send, just send a string: .... Sometimes a higher speed station will substitute just a couple of dits: **DIT DIT   DIT DIT**, or several, widely spaced single dits.

$\overline{VE}$ = After making a sending error, this is sometimes used as sort of a re-set mechanism for the finger-brain connection. Don't ask me why, but it works for me and you'll hear many others using it.

47

Common Procedural Signals

DE = "from" (e.g., **S57WJ DE KR3E**)

ES = "and"

K = Indicates you are turning the conversation over to another station or stations.

KN = Indicates you are turning the conversation over to a specific station and no one else is to call or answer. Use this only when you wish a specific station to answer and when you do not want your QSO to be interrupted by a breaker.

R = All received and understood. The CW version of "roger." You *do not* need to send it more than once. *Do not* send it if you haven't had solid copy on what the other station has sent.

? = In addition to indicating a question, a question mark is frequently used as a substitute for QRZ? It's also used, at times, when you want to indicate that you are repeating something, e.g. **NAME IS NAPOLEON ? NAPOLEON**.

CL = I'm closing my station. This is sent after the final identification. I'm turning off the rig, pulling the switch, going QRT. Don't bother to call me because I'm shutting it all down.

To DIT DIT or Not to DIT DIT?

It's not listed as a pro-sign or a procedural signal, but **DIT DIT** is heard at the end of many CW contacts. It's a final sign-off that, apparently, dates back to the days of ship-to-shore communications using Morse code. Shore operators, who were required to consistently monitor the 500 kHz emergency frequency, might break the boredom by sending a single **DIT**. Another op would respond with **DIT DIT**. Someone else would join in with **DIT DIDIDIT DIT** and another would send **DIT DIT**, matching the rhythm of the old refrain "Shave and a Haircut ... Two Bits."

In the late 1950s and early 1960s this morphed onto the Novice ham bands. Some Novice ops, instead of sending a CQ, would send **DIT DIDIDIT DIT** and wait for someone to answer with **DIT DIT**. The two stations would then send their callsigns and begin a QSO.

Fast-forward to today and a small part of this tradition continues, but at the end of a QSO rather than at the beginning. **DIT DIT** is sent as a friendly: "that's it," I'm really all finished.

Some CW purists rant against this practice, but I've always found it very useful. If I'm waiting for a QSO to end because I want to call one of those stations, but I may not hear both sides of the QSO, I'll listen for something like this: **GL ES 73 $\overline{\text{SK}}$ G3SXW DE WØVTT K**. I can't hear G3SXW, so I can't determine when to call my friend WØVTT without interfering with G3SXW's final transmission. However, knowing that Mike, VTT will probably send a simple **DIT DIT** to acknowledge Roger's final transmission, I wait for that to happen. Hearing **DIT DIT**, I can be reasonably sure that I can now call Mike without "stepping" on Roger.

Q-Signals

Q-signals convey a lot of meaning with just three letters. They can be sent as a statement or a question. Although there is an "official" meaning for each Q-signal, the definitions used here are the way these signals are commonly used on the air:

QRG = The frequency is . . . . What is the frequency (to which we should QSY)?

QRL = This frequency is in use. (Send this if you're using a frequency and you hear someone send QRL?).
Is this frequency in use? (Send this, once or twice, before calling CQ).

QRM = Interference

QRN = Static

QRO = High power

QRP = Low power (usually 5 watts or less)

QRQ = Send faster. May I send faster?

QRS = Please send slower. Should I send slower?

QRT = I'm going off the air.

QRU = I have nothing further to say (send). Do you have anything further to say (send) to me?

QRV = I am ready to receive. Are you ready to receive?

QRX = Please stand-by.

QRZ = Who is calling me? (*Do not* use this in place of "CQ.")

QSB = Your signal is fading. Is my signal fading?

QSK = I can hear you as I send. Feel free to break in. Can you hear me as you send?

QSL = I confirm your message. Will you confirm what I've sent?

QSO = Two stations communicating with each other.

QSP = Please relay a message to (callsign). . . . Will you relay a message to (callsign).

QST = A general call preceding a message addressed to all hams.

QSX = I (or a particular station) am operating "split", i.e., transmitting on one frequency and listening on another.

QSY = I am going to change my frequency to (callsign). Should I (or can you) change frequency to (a specified frequency)?

The RST System

If you've been operating SSB you should be familiar with signal reports. The same system of R = Readability and S = Strength is also used on CW. However, for CW a third report is added: T = Tone. In this day of solid state rigs you may ask, "Why do we do this?" The answer to that question is the same one that the character Tevya gives in the famous Broadway musical "Fiddler on the Roof." Tradition!

When I started in ham radio, over 50 years ago, it wasn't uncommon to hear a CW signal with a tone quality that sounded rough to the ear. It was sort of a buzz, so the tone didn't sound completely pure. Once in a blue moon I'll hear this on the air today, usually from someone who is operating a very old rig or from a station operating in a DX location that has a very poor (unfiltered) electrical system. I think I've given only two or three reports that were less than T-9 over the past 30 years. Why do we bother sending tone reports anymore? I guess for that once-in-a-decade QSO that's less than T9.

Here is the traditional RST chart:

Readability: How well can I hear what you're sending? I might be able to copy you R5 even though your signal strength is very week. Or, due to QRM or QRN, I might only copy R3 even though you are very strong.

1 = Unreadable

2 = Barely readable, occasional words distinguishable

3 = Readable with considerable difficulty

4= Readable with practically no difficulty

5 = Perfectly readable

Signal Strength: You can look at the S-meter on your rig to get an approximate S reading. I usually just judge by what my ear tells me.

1 = Faint signals, barely perceptible

2 = Very weak signals

3 = Weak signals

4 = Fair signals

5 = Fairly good signals

6 = Good signals

7 = Moderately strong signals

8 = Strong signals

9 = Extremely strong signals

Tone:

1: Sixty cycle a.c. or less, very rough and broad

2: Very rough a.c., very harsh and broad

3: Rough a.c. tone, rectified but not filtered

4: Rough tone, some trace of filtering

5: Filtered rectified a.c. but strongly ripple-modulated

6: Filtered tone, definite trace of ripple modulation

7: Near pure tone, trace of ripple modulation

8: Near perfect tone, slight trace of modulation

9: Perfect tone, no trace of ripple or modulation of any kind

If you hear chirp on a signal add a "C" to your report. If you hear key clicks add a "K."

Chapter 5

Let's Take a Trip

"Don't ever get started doing CW mobile. Period. It's a bad habit that you will never be able to stop." –KØRU

CW on the Highway

K5ALU: Red Cranford, K5ALU is a million-miler. Ever since he got his driver's license at age 16, Red has been operating mobile. In fact, it's extremely rare to hear K5ALU operating without /m on the end of his call, and K5ALU is 100% CW.

Since 1994 Red has had five pick-ups, SUVs, or vans and each has had a rig. He logged 932,000 miles on those vehicles and hundreds of thousands more  since he began driving in 1958. His latest shack on wheels is a 2013 Ford F-350 with an Icom 7100, a Scorpion screwdriver antenna mounted on a bar across the truck's bed, and a Vibroplex iambic paddle. Red moved the rubber feet on the bottom of the paddle and glued them to a position that

K5ALU's Vibroplex iambic paddle mounted in a cup holder.

would allow them to fit into an existing slot in the center console of the F-350. In other vehicles he's used strips of 2-inch wide Velcro® to hold the key.

K5ALU/m has operated from 49 states (it's hard to get the pick-up truck to Hawaii) and the District of Columbia. It was in the Nation's Capital that Red made a wrong turn on Pennsylvania

Avenue one day and the large antenna on the pick-up quickly attracted the attention of the uniformed Secret Service officers who guard the White House. After a short explanation, K5ALU/m was put in reverse and Red and his wife Linda were on the road again.

WW9R uses Begali Traveler mounted on his center console.

WW9R: Pat Hoppe, WW9R in Big Bend, Wisconsin also operates from his truck, but Pat uses a different method to mount his Begali Traveler paddle. The paddle is attached to a small piece of Plexiglas®. The Plexiglas is fastened with epoxy to a small length of PVC pipe and that pipe sits in one of the cup holders in the center console. Pat's wrist rests on part of the Plexiglas and his arm rests on the console.

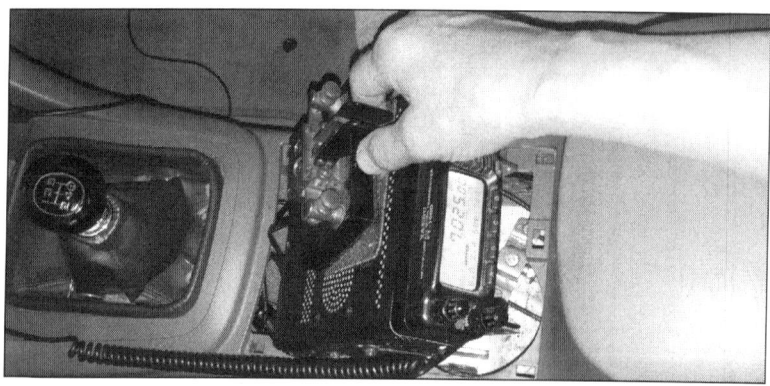

WØVTT mounts his kent paddle vertically.

WØVTT: Mike Cizek, WØVTT locates his paddle, a Kent iambic, in front of the center console of his truck and Mike's key is right on top of his rig. Mike has bolted the mount of his little FT-100 to the console and has fastened the paddle, with its rubber feet removed, directly to the top using heavy-duty Velcro. That positioning allows him to rest his full arm on the center console and he only needs to move his arm and hand a few inches forward to reach his stick shift.

G6PZ: In the U.K., where the right side of the road is the left side, the mounting location for the paddle needs to be different. In his Citroen Expert 2 van, Paul Beecham, G6PZ mounts his paddle on

54

a Perspex (acrylic) base and the base is attached to the driver's arm rest using self-tapping screws. Paul's FT-857 is mounted in a center storage compartment over the cab area with its control head in the center of the dashboard. Like K5ALU, G6PZ has a remote speaker mounted over the driver's seat.

G6PZ's padle on the driver's arm rest.

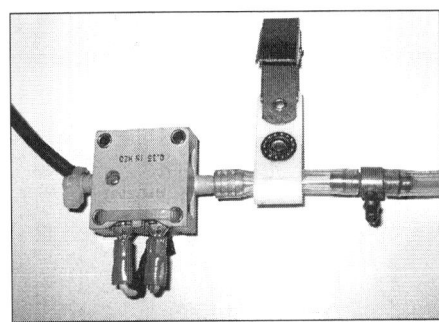

A tube, pressure switch and shirt clip make up the VK6GX pneumatic key.

"Look ma, no hands" when VK6GX ooperates CW mobile.

VK6GX: The award for the most unique mobile key, and probably the safest to use while driving, is the one built and designed by Phil Hartwell, VK6GX. Phil has built a pneumatic "key" that allows him to operate hands-free while on the road. He clamps the device to his shirt collar, grips the tube between his teeth and blows into it as if he's whistling the dits and dahs. A sensitive pressure switch picks up his blowing and acts as a key. Phil has even included a "T" piece to prevent over pressurization of the sensor and to vent moisture.

Tips to Taking CW "On the Road"

As you can see, there are lots of ways to take CW along for the ride.

Operating CW mobile isn't for everyone, and it's certainly not for a beginner, but once you're comfortable copying CW in your mind, and have the ability to mount your rig and key in a comfortable and safe location in your vehicle, it can be a whole lot of fun (as well as a way to get on the air if you live in an antenna-restricted area).

Here are a few tips, with thanks to K5ALU, for enjoying CW on the road:

- Start by just listening for a while as you drive. Don't try to send until you're comfortable copying in your head.
- Don't ever try to write anything, not even calls or names. It's just not safe.
- Don't use headphones. Again, it's not safe; it removes your mind from the road and may block out the sound of an approaching emergency vehicle. In some states wearing headphones also may be illegal. If your companion in the other seat complains about being forced to listen to "all that noise," buy him or her an iPad, include some games and give that person some headphones.
- Use an external speaker and mount it near your ear. That keeps the noise out of the other person's space and closer to you.
- Use a solid paddle that can take a beating. Small "finger" paddles tend to break quickly. A Bencher BY-1, the paddle with a spring, runs the risk of the spring flying off if you hit the paddle with your elbow or wrist.
- Be attentive to the road and your surroundings. If you're in heavy traffic, or worse, in stop-and-go, go QRT. Interstate driving with a cruise control is best.
- Choose your rig carefully. Make sure it's easy to view and easy to reach. If you have to lean down to use the rig you're asking for an accident. The new rigs with control heads, which are light and easy to mount, are great. No need to drill holes … just keep it in place with some 2-inch wide Velcro. A rig with a touch-screen, such as the Icom 7100, is also good.
- Very detailed information about operating mobile can be found on the www.k0bg.com web site.

CW on the Sea

Cars and trucks aren't the only mode of transportation that you can you use to have CW mobiling fun. Operating from a cruise ship can be a real blast and, in most cases, CW (or a digital mode) is the only way to do that.

Princess is one example of the cruise lines that allow ham operation. Not surprisingly, you need to notify them in advance and there are restrictions. They include limiting your power to less than 25 watts and your antenna to a vertical that's no longer than 5 feet. You're not going to do very well with that setup on SSB, but with the help of your salt water "front yard," running QRP with a small antenna can be more than enough to work lots of DX on CW.

G6PZ's set-up in his cabin on the cruise ship Aurora.

G6PZ: In addition to operating from his Citroen van, G6PZ has operated on four cruise ships from three different cruise lines. According to Paul, "CW is the most successful mode to date. SSB is anti-social as you can upset people around you with unwanted noise. Data is OK but it's much more pleasurable to work CW."

Paul uses an IC 7000 with its remote aerial coupler feeding a telescopic glass fiber fishing pole with a wire running through it. His earth ground was direct from the coupler to the ship's deck using a small G clamp. The pole is secured to the guard rail with elastic bungee type rope. He's also used a mobile whip clamped to the cabin's balcony railing.

For CW operation Paul recommends a quiet paddle, such as a touch type.

N1RA: For a cruise ship, CW operator Bob Avrutik, N1RA modified a Bencher BY-1 paddle by removing its heavy base and, using

N1RA with his shack-on-a-ship.

it as a template, drilled matching holes in a 1/8" x 3" x 3-3/4" plastic plate. Four suction cups as legs were added to keep it from sliding. Bob says this made a tremendous reduction in the weight of the key and it was a pleasure for him to use.

Cruising Tips:

- Obtain a letter from the cruise line of your choice giving you permission to operate aboard the ship and *be sure to bring it with you.*

- Also bring copies of
    - the CEPT Treaty (reciprocal licensing)
    - a list of the ITU Regions and their operating frequencies
    - a copy of the bill of sale for the radio equipment in case US Customs or airport security has any questions about the origin of the equipment

- Plan to use a paper log so you don't have to lug a laptop with you.

CQing on Top of the World

Well, maybe not quite that high, but when Fred Maas, **KT5X**, John De Primo, **K1JD**, and others who operate from mountain peaks as part of the Summits On The Air program call CQ at 13,000 feet above sea level they probably feel like that's where they are.

CW is the mode of choice for SOTA work for many of the same reasons that Fred and John enjoy it in their shacks: CW is simple,

AD5A using a KX-3 with built-in paddle at about 9,400 ft. in New Mexico.

lightweight gear and narrower bandwidth means it gets through better than SSB under marginal conditions. Of course, according to K1JD, another necessary component is a good level of ability on the part of the ham using the key.

Here are the two setups that John has used for his summiting work:

Number 1: Elecraft KX3 w/internal tuner, KX3 paddle, Shure earbuds, homebrew 9:1 UNUN in a small floss container with 2mm female connector and 5-foot RG-174 coax terminated with a male BNC, 42-foot wire with 2mm male connector, 4.5AH LiFePO4 12.8v battery with jumper to KX3, internal NiMH batteries in the KX3 (backup power), LL Bean Pack with one water bottle. This setup has been used, for example, on Hermit Peak: 8 miles round trip, 2,700-foot elevation gain.

Number 2: ATS-4A, AME Mini-B paddle, LiPo battery (500 mah, 1300 mah depending on number of activations), Sennheiser earbuds, homebrew BNC-BNC 6-foot jumper with Teflon® coax, Hendricks end-fed half-wave (EFHW) tuner with female 2mm connector, 66-foot ended wire with 2mm male connector plus 2mm jumpers within the wire to make 7, 10, 14, and 21 MHz half-wave antennas. CamelBak Mule pack with 3-liter water bladder. This setup was used, for example, on Santa Fe Baldy, 15 miles round trip and 2400-foot elevation gain.

Common components: 21-foot carbon fiber fishing rod to support the antenna, bungie cord for securing the pole to a shrub or anything available, figure 8 winder for the wire, very basic first aid kit.

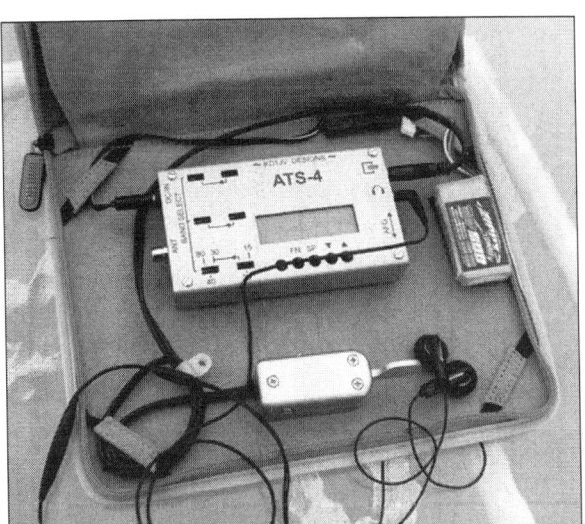

Suitcase shack used by K1JD to put summits on the air.

It's all about having fun

Of course you don't have to hike up a mountain to enjoy off-the-road CW. The small size of many rigs, plus the more-bang-for-the-watts factor, makes CW a natural anywhere you travel.

CW can be a lot of fun and rewarding no matter where you operate, be it on the road, on the sea, from a mountaintop, or wherever you travel. Just be sure you have the appropriate equipment to do the job, follow the rules of wherever you take your mobile CW station, be safe, and have fun!

TF/S53R operates CW while camping near the sea in Corsica. Robert is using an IC746PRO feeding 15 feet of coax into 60 feet of wire.

Chapter 6

CW Gave Them a Voice

Steve Harper first learned Morse code when he was 11 years old. Since then he's used it every day of his life. Steve's not a ham, nor does he work in radio communications, but CW is his voice to the world.

Steve was born with severe Cerebral Palsy and has never been able to speak.

In 1979, however, he became one of five, non-verbal children who participated in project at the University of Washington that would change his life. The children in this project would learn to "speak" by learning Morse code. Once they accomplished that, all were given "communicators," devices similar to code practice oscillators. But instead of being connected to a hand key or a paddle, Steve's communicator was connected to two switches, one on either side of his head. Similar to using a paddle, Steve would tilt his head to one side to send dits and the other side to send dahs. Steve says it took him about two weeks to learn the code and another year to become good at sending it.

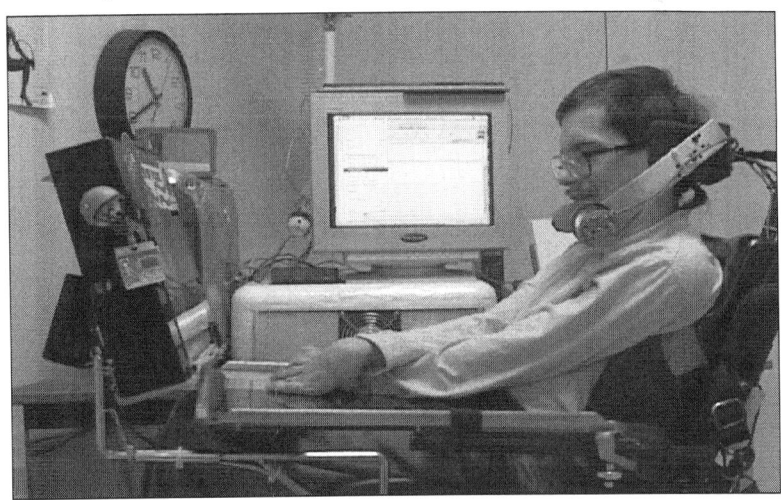

Steve Harper speaking by using Morse Code.

Using his Morse code setup, Steve graduated high school and college. He went on to become webmaster for a firm in the Seattle area where he did most of his "speaking" using a MacBook Pro. Today he manages the database for a Seattle area firm. You can watch Steve speaking with Morse code at: http://www.youtube.com/watch?v=0ZQRRogNepM

There have been hospital patients who, unable to speak due to an illness or accident, have used Morse code to communicate. In an article written in 1992 for *QST* magazine, Dr. Dennis Ross, K6DR tells the story of a retired ship's radio operator who was unable to speak after suffering a stroke. While making rounds, Dr. Ross, then a medical student, heard a patient tapping on his bedside table with a spoon. He quickly realized that it was the stroke patient and he was using CW, sent with a spoon, as his voice. The patient told Dr. Ross that he felt like he was trapped in a radio shack with a working receiver but a broken transmitter. Soon, Dr. Ross set up a Vibroplex® bug and a code oscillator. "Harry never regained his ability to speak," wrote Dr. Ross, "but he was verbose in Morse code."[1]

A ham friend in the U.K., who worked as a physiotherapist in a top London hospital, had a similar experience. One weekend a patient was admitted who was immobile and unable to speak. The medical staff had trouble communicating with him. Learning that the patient had once been a communications officer in the Royal Navy, the U.K. ham took the patient's hand and tapped CQ. My friend said there was general bemusement at the next ward meeting when my pal told everyone the patient was comfortable and could hear and comprehend everything that was being said around him. The patient also tapped out in code: "I don't like…" and "I don't mind having a bed bath from "X" with the big …!"

Perhaps the most dramatic use of Morse code off the air was by Jeremiah Denton. Held prisoner during the Vietnam War, Commander Denton blinked "T O R T U R E" in Morse code when his North Vietnamese captors forced him to appear in a Japanese television interview. It was the first confirmation of North Vietnamese atrocities during the war. You can see part of that interview on YouTube: **https://www.youtube/BgelmcOdS38**

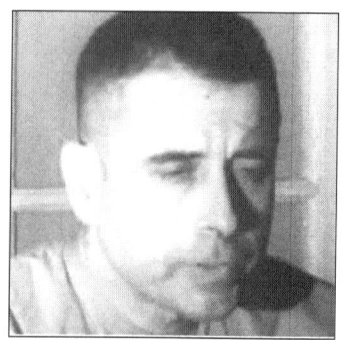

Cmdr. Jeremiah Denton Jr. uses his eyes to blink a Morse Code message.

[1] Ross, "Morse Code: A Place in the Mind"

Chapter 7

It's Old But It's Still New

I t was 1825. Samuel Morse's wife had been ill and, while on a trip to Washington, DC, Morse received a letter from his father with news that Morse's wife had suddenly passed away. However, the letter traveled slowly and by the time Morse received it and then traveled back to his hometown of New Haven, Connecticut Susan Walker Morse had already been buried. After that Morse was determined to find a way to communicate information that traveled faster than the mail.

By 1836 Morse had invented a way to do that. He would accomplish it by sending long and short electrical pulses along a wire, using a simple code. Morse demonstrated his invention to the U.S. Congress in 1844 by sending the famous message "What hath God wrought" on a wire

This key is believed to be from the first Baltimore-Washington telegraph line. Photo by Smithsonian Institution.

that ran along the railroad tracks between Washington, DC and Baltimore. Morse's language of long and short pulses, dots and dashes, would come to be known as the Morse code. Could Samuel Morse have imagined all of the ways that his code would be used over the next two centuries?

News

In 1848, news of the Mexican War was received by Americans within hours of battles, thanks, in part, to Morse code. Also that

63

Associated Press telegraphers on the New York "cable desk" around 1920. (AP photo).

year, the Associated Press used the telegraph to receive presidential voting results from the 36 states that then existed. In 1899 AP married with Morse code and CW to cover the America's Cup yacht race off Sandy Hook, New Jersey. By 1923, nearly 1,500 Morse operators linked about 1,000 newspapers with AP's news bureaus around the world. According to Aubrey Keel, KBØZE (SK), who was the last surviving AP telegrapher, all of the telegraphers used bugs, mostly Vibroplexes, and sent at about 30 words per minute. AP continued to use telegraphy to relay its news stories until 1933.

Telegrams

Morse code, of course, made it possible for people to send birthday greetings, requests for money, and other personal messages

Samuel Morse sends a final message on telegraph circuits at event honoring him in June 1871,

via telegraph. Telegrams were most popular in the 1920s and 30s, when sending one was less expensive than making a transcontinental phone call.

Maritime Radio

On the seas, CW with Morse code was a lifesaver.

In December 1898, the East Goodwin Lightship, anchored off the coast of England, was struck by another ship in a thick fog. The lightship used Morse code to send what is believed to be the first distress signal from a ship. Help was quickly sent and both ships were secured.

The first time an American ship sent a CW distress message was in 1905, when another light ship, Relief Ship 58, sent "help" as it floundered off Nantucket, Massachusetts. A naval radio station in Rhode Island heard the message and sent help. Ten minutes after the light ship's crew was transferred to a rescue ship, Relief Ship 58 went under.

One of the last SOSs sent from a ship was sent in February 1987. Radio operator John Davies, 9V1VV heard it in his radio shack aboard the Supertanker Eriskay. John told his story on www.maritime.org, the web site of the Maritime Radio Historical Society:

> *I was on board the VLCC Eriskay going north to Japan in heavy monsoon seas, somewhere south of the Straits of Taiwan. I received an SOS on 500KHz from New Concord - a small general cargo ship on her maiden voyage, loaded with logs. She had taken a heavy roll and the cargo shifted, making her list badly and slowly taking in water through the hatch covers. Apparently they had been trying to bail out using pumps for 36 hours to no avail. We were very close and within two hours we were in position upwind of her, using our fully laden bulk to give her some lee while they abandoned ship in an open lifeboat. 16 guys all rowing for their lives!*
>
> *The odd thing about this rescue was that once the survivors were safely on board we received a distress relay on Satcom A - far too late. It was all over by then. I had relayed the SOS to the nearby coast station at Khaohsiung (Taiwan) and it was picked up by several vessels in the area as well.*

During the golden age of maritime communications, stations stretched along sea coasts around the world, each with its own

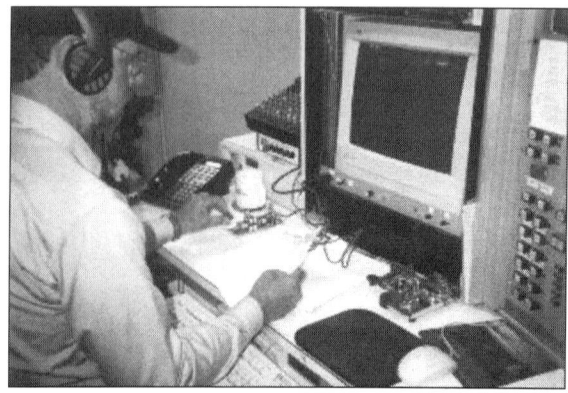

Richard "RD" Dilllman, W6AWO sends one of the final messages from maritime statiions KFS and KPH. (Photo: Maritime Radio Historical Society.)

area of coverage and call sign. Although they monitored for emergency communications, their primary duty was to send and receive routine message traffic.

Over the years, the use of CW in the maritime was replaced by voice and satellite communications. Slowly, CW maritime stations went silent. And, on July 13, 1999, at 0059 UCT, after 87 years of service, coastal station KFS in Point Reyes, California sent the final dits and dahs:

CQ DE KFS THIS IS THE FINAL CW TRANSMISSION FROM STATION KFS - THE LAST COMMERCIAL RADIOTELEGRAPH STATION IN NORTH AMERICA. APPROPRIATELY, WE CLOSE CW AND EMBARK ON A NEW ERA OF COMMUNICATION WITH SAMUEL F.B. MORSE'S WORDS OF 155 YEARS AGO BT NW CL 73 BT WHAT HATH GOD WROUGHT BT DE KFS SK

On The Rails

Keeping the trains on time was made easier, and safer, as Morse code allowed railway telegraphers to relay word of arrivals and departures along the route and to change train orders.

In 1851 the first such order, a message changing the meeting point between two trains, was sent on the Erie railroad. As documented in the book *Between the Ocean*

Railroad telegraph operator A.L. Krenke at work in the Santa Fe Depot. (San Diego Union-Tribune).

66

and the Lakes, by William H. Steward, the message was: "To Agent and Operator at Goshen: Hold the train for further orders, signed, Charles Minot, Superintendent." It wasn't long before other railroads began using the telegraph to coordinate train movements.

WW II recruiting poster.

Military

Abraham Lincoln had a staff of four telegraphers during the Civil War and used Morse code to communicate directly with generals on the battlefield. In the 20th century, CW was used wherever other modes of communication were impractical, as well as for sending "coded" messages. The CW mode was simple and efficient.

In early 2005, the Department of Defense pulled the switch on CW, sending out a message stating there was no longer a need for operators to be trained in Morse code as a specialty.

Old Beats New

Despite the military and commercial services migrating to other communication modes, and the popularity today of things such texting and Twittering, Samuel Morse's code lives on as one of the fastest and most reliable ways to communicate.

In 2005, *The Tonight Show with Jay Leno* put

Chip Margelli, K7JA races text-messaging champ Ben Cook on the Tonight Show, May 13, 2005.

text messaging and Morse code to a head-to-head race. CW operators Chip Margelli, K7JA and Ken Miller, K6CTW faced off against world text-messaging champ Ben Cook of Utah and his friend Jason. Neither team knew, in advance, the message they would send: "I just saved a bunch of money on my car insurance." Using a Bencher paddle, Margelli sent the message to Miller at 29 words per minute, while Cook used his phone keyboard to send a text message. (You can see the contest on YouTube at: https://youtu.be/pRuRE-Bwk1U)

It comes to no surprise for any CW operator that the winner of that contest was the team using CW and Morse code, K7JA and K6CTW. No doubt, Samuel Morse would be pleased.

To This Day . . .

Morse code continues to be an important part of ham radio and other communication. It's flashed the news, saved lives and, for many, it's simply been "music" to their ears... providing countless hours of pleasure. Come join the adventure.

Appendix I

The DX Code of Conduct

- I will listen, and listen, and then listen again before calling.

- I will only call if I can copy the DX station properly.

- I will not trust the DX cluster and will be sure of the DX station's call sign before calling.

- I will not interfere with the DX station nor anyone calling and will never tune up on the DX frequency or in the QSX slot.

- I will wait for the DX station to end a contact before I call.

- I will always send my full call sign.

- I will call and then listen for a reasonable interval. I will not call continuously.

- I will not transmit when the DX operator calls another call sign, not mine.

- I will not transmit when the DX operator queries a call sign not like mine.

- I will not transmit when the DX station requests geographic areas other than mine.

- When the DX operator calls me, I will not repeat my call sign unless I think he has copied it incorrectly.

- I will be thankful if and when I do make a contact.

- I will respect my fellow hams and conduct myself so as to earn their respect.

Find more information at: **http://www.dx-code.org/**

Appendix II

CW Clubs

- **AGCW** – German CW club **www.agcw.org**

- **CTC** - Croation Telegraph Club **www.cw-ctc.com**

- **CWOps** – International CW club and CW Academy **www.cwops.org**

- **CW Operators' QRP Club** –Australian based QRP CW club **www.vkqrpclub.org**

- **First Class CW Operators Club** - British-based international CW club **www.g4foc.org**

- **FISTS** –International CW club with many beginning level members **www.fists.org**

- **GACW** - Argentinian CW club **www.gacw.org**

- **HSC** – High Speed Telegraphy Club **www.morsecode.nl**

- **Morse Telegraph Club** - Perpetuates the knowledge and traditions of telegraphy and American Morse Code. **www.morsetelegraphclub.org/**

- **RCWC** - Russian CW Club **http://rcwc.net**

- **SKCC** – Straight Key Century Club, dedicated to operating mechanical keys **www.skccgroup.com**